TAMAR'S VOICE

A Journey from a Sexual Assault Victim to a Survivor

Samantha Payne

TAMAR'S VOICE

Published by
Kingdom Kaught Publishing, LLC
Denton, Maryland, USA

Edited by Frank L. Holloman

Cover Design by Agape Advertisement, Inc.

ISBN: 978-0-9964040-0-6

Library of Congress Control Number (LCCN): 2015942400

Tamar's Voice

This book is designed to help those who have experienced sexual assault in any form, be it rape, molestation, or any other type of sexual assault. In this book, I share my own personal process of healing as I describe and outline the emotional journey I went through during my fight to become a survivor. This book can be read from front to back or the table of contents can be used to find particular chapters to address specific feelings. My prayer is that victims will receive healing and begin their own personal journey towards becoming a survivor.

For those that have lost their voice and suffer in silence.

Acknowledgments

This book would have never been completed without the assistance from some important people. First and foremost, to my publisher and graphic designer, Bishop Antonio Palmer, thank you for the time and effort put into "Tamar's Voice".

To my editor, Pastor Frank, thank you for spending long hours to make my thoughts coherent.

To Mrs. Barbara Palmer, Angelica, Jamice, Takiya, and Zenda thank you all for inspiring me to develop a closer relationship with God.

To my husband, Dewayne, and my children Khari and Aniyah I want to express my love and gratitude for your moral support.

To those that have entrusted me with their story, I am honored and thank you for encouraging me to write this book.

To my parents Samuel, Carla, and Domestra, other family members, and friends who have encouraged me through hard times, thank you for reminding me that I will overcome in spite of my circumstances.

To my brothers, Keith and Kenny, thank you for believing in me no matter what and pushing me to be the best me that I can be.

Lastly but always first, I thank God for His patience and loving me.

Table of Contents

My Story

"You intended to harm me, but God intended it for good to accomplish what is now being done, the saving of many lives"
Genesis 50:21.

Many years ago God put it on my heart to write a book about rape. Since I never aspired to be an author, I simply discarded the thought. As the years passed, the concept of the book continued to come up in conversations with various people. During my period of resistance, I continued to ask God, "Why?" Throughout my adult life I pursued various ministries... I volunteered at homeless shelters, sung on praise teams and choirs, and taught a few bible classes but the book remained unwritten.

Over time, I met more and more people that were victims of sexual assault like I had been. I would always let them know that I could relate to their plight and if our relationship got a little closer, then I would also tell them about this book that I was supposed to have written. They would always respond with, if you write it, I will read it.

The voices of other victims along with the voice of God finally resonated in my head and pushed me forward with the book again. I originally attempted to do research on the topic of rape to write this book but I was still a little uncomfortable and really did not know exactly what to write. Through my academic experiences, having been a teacher and a college student for a couple of years, I was initially writing this book like a research paper but found myself bored while I typed and so the book still remained unwritten.

Then one day out of the blue, a friend of mine told me I had been on her mind. Little did I know, she had begun a ministry and was co-sponsoring a cell group of the 40-Day Surrender Fast by Celeste Owens. As she talked, I knew the conversation we were having was the answer to the prayer I had petitioned God about a few weeks prior. At the time I asked God for increased accountability. I also told Him I was tired of doing the work for Him. Lastly I added that I wanted to do and was ready to do whatever He wanted me to do.

I began to feel that just doing what I was comfortable doing for God was no longer enough. I needed to begin to truly surrender my life to Him and to follow His will for my life, especially since there were already so many things that He had done for me. During the fast, I realized I had been attacking this book-writing task completely wrong... the book was not designed to be a research paper!

After reading the first chapter of the pre-fast devotional in the 40-Day Surrender Fast, I realized that the author actually wrote how she talked. Then the light bulb came on for me... writing this book requires my 'voice'! The journey I had been on is just that, my journey. I know that others, who have experienced sexual assault, have taken a completely different journey than mine but my prayer is that all can relate to my story and receive some measure of healing and restoration.

What follows is an unadulterated account of my life story from a sexual assault victim to a survivor:

I have had some extremely traumatic experiences occur in my life. I have been raped by 3 different men and sexually assaulted by others. The first time I was raped I was a virgin. It was the summer of my freshman year in high school. I had a boyfriend and thought I was starting to grow out of being some nerdy, overlooked little girl. He asked if he could come over to my house. Prior to his visit, we agreed to just kiss but instead of stopping at a kiss he started to tug on my pants. I began to squirm and ask him what he was doing.

The next thing I knew I felt a terrible pain and all I could do was muster up a meek, "No, no I don't want this." My boyfriend raped me on my living room floor. Not only did that boy take my virginity, he also took my dignity and my youth from me. I felt guilty and dirty for what happened to me. I took a shower but could not seem to get clean enough. Not only that, I also felt lonely because I was scared to tell anyone what happened to me.

Over time I slowly put what happened in the back of my mind. Now 4 years later it was the summer of my freshman year of college. It was the week before classes actually started and Thursdays were the party days at my new school. There was an off-campus party this particular night and I saw a girl from my dorm getting in a car with 3 guys. She asked me to go with her. Although I really did not want to go, all I could think about was how bad I would feel if something happened to her.

We got to a music store which doubled as a house. Everyone was drinking alcohol and some people were smoking. I was uncomfortable but stayed to support the girl from my dorm. Then the music suddenly stopped playing. One of the guys told me the music plays from the inside and asked me if I wanted to pick out the next CD to play. Thinking nothing of it and knowing there were other people in the house, I agreed.

As soon as we got by the CD player he threw me on the ground and raped me on the floor of the store. I even heard someone come out of their room because they heard the struggle but whoever it was simply closed their door and pretended not to see what was happening. It was like I did not matter nor was I worth the time or the effort to save me from the attack.

Even worse, after everything was over, I went outside and found out that the girl I was looking out for had left me there alone. I walked back to campus alone, crying, and angry!

I was angry at the girl for asking me to go with her and then leaving me. I was angry with the person that ignored my cries for help and I was especially angry at the man who violated me. This incident also caused me to flashback to what happened to me when I was younger. I had apparently been suffering from PTSD throughout my high school years and so now, there I was a freshman in college, dealing with two incidences of rape. I felt worthless, dirty, and fearful. I wanted to transfer schools or somehow magically disappear. The pain was too much to handle and I did not know where to turn.

Before my freshman year was over, I met a guy who was very knowledgeable about the Bible. Eventually I ended up confiding in him and told him what had happened to me. He continued to listen and told me of his plans to start a Bible study on campus. I was comforted by reading the Bible and excited about my new friendship. The friendship later turned into something more and we started dating and were partners in the ministry he started on campus. He graduated soon after but I still had some time before I was scheduled to graduate. He ended up proposing to me because he decided God was telling him we were supposed to get married. I somehow missed the memo but I trusted his judgment.

We ended up getting married but at the onset there were a lot of people who were against it for a variety of reasons. For one, I was only 19 at the time. Additionally, apparently others could readily see that he was very controlling. Those on the outside obviously had the gift of discernment because while he tried to make it seem that we were a model couple, in reality the relationship was extremely rocky. Nevertheless I was convinced that all relationships had troubles like ours; however, it turns out that I was wrong. In fact, even before we were married, he would force me to have sex with him then after we were married, I was still forced to have sex, which by definition constitutes a rape because a relationship status does not change what rape truly is.

The very person I trusted violated my trust and my body. This man whom I married was supposed to be a minister of God so how could he hurt me in this manner. I felt confused, worthless, and weak because now I had been a victim 3 times. I did not know how I was going to make it through to the next day and sometimes I did not want to continue to live. It was a struggle for many years. During this time, I also became confused about my relationship with God. I no longer wanted to read my Bible and only went to church periodically when someone invited me to go.

I eventually regained the desire to revive my relationship with God but I was ashamed I had turned my back on Him. I was also ashamed of all of the detours I had taken in my life without God. One day I attended a Bible study at someone's home with a friend in Texas. On the first day of the Bible study, the teacher said something so simple yet so profound for me at that point in my life. She told us that God loves us and all He wants is a personal, intimate relationship with us. All of my confusion dissipated and I immediately started to pursue a closer relationship with God.

At that very moment all the confusion I had was gone and the feelings of worthlessness I had disappeared. I believed what she said was true and ever since then, I have been walking with God... I have also been in the process of healing and transforming from a victim to a survivor of sexual assault.

Since not many people know my story, I find it amusing that when they see me bubbling with joy, they oftentimes feel the need to remark that life is not all lollipops and rainbows like it has been for me. I chuckle because they don't know that I have been through the trenches and back and then back again. I do not even think that most people would wish the experiences I have gone through in my short lifetime on their enemies.

However, I have relied on God for my strength because He is the only One who could have pulled me out of the mess I have encountered. Despite what has happened to me, I truly have plenty I can be grateful for in my life.

Tamar's Story

"Tamar put ashes on her head and tore the ornate robe she was wearing. She put her hands on her head and went away, weeping aloud as she went. Her brother Absalom said to her, 'Has that Amnon, your brother, been with you? Be quiet for now, my sister; he is your brother. Don't take this thing to heart.' And Tamar lived in her brother Absalom's house, a desolate woman"

2 Samuel 13:19-20.

In 1999, after I was raped the second time, I started reading through the entire Bible and came across a story in 2 Samuel, Chapter 13 where a woman by the name of Tamar had been raped. I was surprised that this story did not sound familiar to me because I basically grew up in church but had never heard her story before. Tamar's father was King David, who was a man in the Bible known for chasing after God's own heart amongst other things. David had an older son named Amnon. He later fathered Tamar and her brother Absalom with another one of his wives, Maacah.

When the children grew older, Amnon fell in love with his half-sister, Tamar. He conspired with his uncle Shimeah to devise a plan to give him an opportunity to be alone with Tamar. Amnon pretended to be sick and asked his father, King David, if his sister Tamar could be the one to care for him. She is obedient to her father's request. Now when she gets to Amnon's sleeping quarters, he sends all of the servants out of the room.

He asks her to feed him personally. She obeys but then he rapes her. In the midst of the incident, Tamar still tries to reason with her half-brother by asking him to just marry her, so no sin would be committed. Amnon refuses, rapes her, and then forces her to leave because he despised her even more than he lusted after her in the beginning. Tamar was punished for her obedience to her father and to her brother and then treated as though she had done something wrong.

After she leaves Amnon's bedroom, Tamar puts ashes on her head, which in those times meant she was mourning, and she cries out. Absalom finds out what has happened to his sister and he takes her into his home. The Bible relays that Tamar goes to live in Absalom's home and becomes a desolate woman, meaning she was empty. The Bible records nothing more of Tamar after she was raped. Naturally King David also finds out about the incident and is angry but nothing is done for Tamar. Absalom feels that something should be done so he devises a plan to have Amnon killed in the years to come.

A couple of years later, while Absalom and a group of his brothers including Amnon were in the wilderness, he instructs the servants to get Amnon drunk and then to kill him. After Amnon was killed, all of the other brothers left. Later King David received a report that Absalom had killed Amnon and he grieved. Then the same uncle, Shimeah, reminds King David of what Amnon had done! Absalom went into hiding after his brother Amnon was killed.

In the end Amnon honored his sister by naming his own daughter Tamar. I also want to honor Tamar by naming my book after her. This is because Tamar's story was all too familiar to me. I want to give her the voice she lost when she was raped. When a person has been raped, they often feel the same way Tamar did, thinking their life is over once they have been violated. In Tamar's situation, she did absolutely nothing wrong and the same holds true for all other rape victims. Tamar was obedient to her father's orders and was a servant to her brother when she was under the impression that he was ill. She did everything she was supposed to do, so why did she have to be the one to suffer in the end?

From Tamar's story we can learn that it is easy to think that your life is over if you have been sexually assaulted. However, that is not the choice you have to make. No matter what happens to you, you still have a voice! You do not have to go into hiding or feel alone nor feel that your life no longer has any purpose. With God you can move beyond your past and walk into the true destiny He has for you.

My Journey

After Tamar was raped she, like so many victims today including me when I was violated, no longer had a voice. A few years ago, I watched a video on sexual assault and in the video there was a young lady who said she was no longer a victim of sexual assault but she was now a survivor. From that video, I realized it was important to look at what happened to me and recognize that I was no longer a victim nor should I continue to be victimized by the feelings I had about the rapes. It was significant to proclaim and declare that I was now a survivor!

There have been times when I tried counseling. After my counseling sessions, the counselors would always comment that I was handling everything perfectly but I did not understand how they could come up with such a conclusion, considering I was hurting so badly internally. To be fair, counselors are not all bad, I just never found one that could help me, and so then I turned to friends and family for help. The response family and friends gave me always seemed to end up with them telling me what a strong person I was. They would reassure me and tell me that they knew I would be fine and would get through any obstacle placed in front of me. I appreciated their confidence in me but did not feel I could make it. I personally never felt strong and now I felt like I was dying on the inside. It became clear to me that my situation was set up so that I would only have God to depend on in order to get healing for what happened to me.

Throughout the years God has shown me how to heal from the deep, inflicted wounds of sexual assault. He has shown me that I am no longer a victim but that I am a survivor in Him. Writing this book makes me feel vulnerable but my goal is to be transparent because I want other victims of sexual assault to know I can relate to how they may be feeling. I am not a counselor but I want people to know about how God is healing and restoring me. This is my personal journey, these are the feelings I have felt, and these are the scriptures that I meditated on, which ultimately led me from being a sexual assault victim to a survivor.

It is Not Your Fault

After I was raped, one of the most difficult aspects for me to deal with was how there were times when I felt that what happened to me was my fault. I would constantly think about how things perhaps could have turned out differently if I would not have been in a particular situation or had not worn a certain revealing outfit or whatever the case may have been.

Unfortunately, during annual training for my job, there is usually at least one person who feels sexual assault is the victim's fault. This is called 'victim blaming' and it is damaging to a victim who may already be blaming themselves. It is completely wrong to shift the blame from the assailant to the victim. This misguided opinion shows a lack of education regarding assaults and is 100% inaccurate. Sexual assault is never the victim's fault!

Again, looking at Tamar's story in the Bible, the only 'mistake' she made was being too beautiful. It is preposterous to think that a woman's beauty makes a sexual assault committed against her, her fault. Tamar's brother wanted what he wanted and he was willing to get it by any means necessary, even if it meant he had to be dishonest with his own father, King David. What happened to Tamar was not her fault. Furthermore, even though he was the one who sent her to her brother's room, it was not her father's fault either. The blame belongs squarely on the perpetrator! Can we all take precautions? Of course but sometimes people have intentions that are unknown and evil in nature. Therefore, it is never the victim's fault and they should never believe nor be made to believe that they caused any type of sexual assault committed against them.

From Confusion to Clarity

"For my thoughts are not your thoughts, neither are your ways my ways,"
declares the LORD.
Isaiah 55:8

The moment after I was raped, I was very confused. I did not know what I was going to do, if I was going to tell anyone, or why this had to happen to me. While I cried in the shower, trying to wash off any residue of my attackers, and with tears streaming down my face, I cried out to God but initially heard nothing in response.

I also reached out to people I thought were close to me and told them what happened but they pretty much blew me off. These were the very same people I had been there for in the past. Whenever they had approached me with anything, I immediately dropped everything to come to their rescue.

16

However, now that I needed someone, I found myself completely alone and without anyone who wanted to make a sacrifice for me.

I did not know what or who to turn to. I just wanted the pain burning inside of me to go away. Because it was so hard to wake up in the morning and continue with my day as if nothing had happened, I felt like I should possibly turn to drugs or even other men to help muffle the pain. I did try alcohol briefly but drinking only made me feel worse. Once I sobered up, I realized the hangovers made getting drunk to ease my pain counterproductive.

The days got harder and I distanced myself more and more from those around me, especially since I felt I had no support anyway. Afterwards, I seemed to gravitate more towards men as my friends and confidants. Unfortunately, I was constantly accused of having some type of sexual relationship with these male friends, which made my heart harden even more. It felt as if I was always misunderstood and that I was being judged based solely on assumptions.

My feelings of confusion soon began to affect my grades in school and how I felt about myself overall. I did not know what direction I should go in. I could not even decide what major to pursue and eventually ended up with 5 different majors while in college, which ultimately prolonged my graduation date an additional semester. It was a very hard time and to make matters worse, I was doing it all alone. I felt alone until one day I was persuaded by a friend to sit down and read the Bible. I was hesitant at first because I never really understood the Bible when I read it alone. The 'thees' and 'thous' in the King James Version of the Bible made it difficult to follow. Then that same friend recommended I try the New International Version (NIV) just to see if I could get a better understanding of the Scriptures.

As I read God's Word, I realized that even though I 'felt' alone, God had been there with me the whole time. This new version truly helped. Now as I read the stories in the Bible, I was able to more readily recognize God's love. I was also able to see that no matter how we try to avoid them, sometimes bad things do happen to us simply because we live in this world.

I read of the reactions of the many saints listed in the Bible. They praised and loved God anyhow, even through their difficult circumstances. Initially it did not make sense to me because I was cursing God for allowing some terrible things to have happened to me. I turned my back on Him because I felt He had turned His back on me. However, when I read the Bible, I realized that God was with me the entire time even through those situations I endured.

When I read the story of Jesus, I saw where He even asked God if there was any other way that we could be saved outside of Him dying on the cross. This was a man that had never sinned and He was killed on the cross so we could be saved. God said no, so Jesus had to endure His fate in order for people to receive salvation, in order for me to receive salvation. He loved me that much - to have the ability to get out of the ultimate sacrifice of death, yet He chose to press on for me. It became clear to me that the least that I could do was to love Him back for the rest of my life and to serve Him with my whole heart.... I had gained a newfound clarity about our relationship.

From Guilty to Blameless

"You shall be blameless before the Lord your God."
Deuteronomy 18:13

When my dignity was taken away from me, some of my initial feelings were guilt and shame. I felt I had done something wrong. I would replay what happened to me over in my head to see where I could have done something different to change the outcome. I truly believed that there was something I could have done differently which would have prevented what someone else did to me.

I focused on things such as what I was wearing, how flirtatious I was with the predators, and how much alcohol I drank on those particular days. I felt I must have done something wrong because out of all of the women my perpetrators could have chosen, they each chose me... So the problem must be me... There must be something wrong with me.

These feelings of mine stemmed from the fact that I had heard other people talk negatively about women when something bad happened to them. I noticed how people always seemed to make statements about the women victims, saying things like "they deserved what happened to them because if they had not been in a particular place then what happened to them would have not have happened". Due to these types of comments, I felt that I could not share what happened to me because I was the one to blame. I began to believe that my actions, leading up to the actual act, caused someone to rape me.

Furthermore, this was something that did not just happen to me once but it happened a second time. After the second time, I felt even worse, believing that I should have "known better." I must be doing something wrong if I am a target for perpetrators. I never considered the fact that maybe my attackers had a problem within themselves.

The feelings of guilt and shame made me feel like I wanted to crawl into a little hole and never come out again. Making matters worse, as people found out about what happened to me, some seemed to question me and treat me differently, as if it were my fault. It could have been that they did not know how to handle such a sensitive topic but in my vulnerable state, I took it personally.

I no longer wanted to participate in my normal activities for fear of the judgment of those around me. People continuously asked what was wrong and seemed genuine but I felt uncomfortable and retreated further and further into my shell. Since I felt like I was being judged, I thought I might as well start doing things that were considered bad like promiscuity, drinking, and drugs so people would at least have a good reason to feel the way they did about me... I might as well give them something to judge me for and not let it be based on any inaccurate assumptions. However, acting out only made me feel worse.

Then I would start to replay what happened to me over again. I faced the feelings of guilt over whether I had fought hard enough to stop the rape or whether I should have been in a particular environment in the first place then perhaps I would have been saved from all of this pain. These feelings of guilt have also been the primary reasons for my silence until now. I did not want to disclose the deep dark secrets of what happened to me because of the fear of the judgment I would receive.

Unfortunately, the feelings of guilt also led me down a path of failing to perform the best I could in other areas of my life. One day I was watching a weight loss show on television and saw that I could truly relate to one of the contestants. One of the trainers on the show felt that this particular contestant was not putting forth the effort she needed to in order to meet the goals of the team. When the trainer went and spoke with the young lady alone, he simply asked her why she was trying to lose the weight. The contestant said that it was for her child, especially since the decisions she made during her pregnancy adversely affected her youngest daughter's health. She went on to say that she felt she was no different from her own mother who had abused her as a child.

Her mother had been a drug abuser and anytime someone complimented her as a child, her mother would hit her in the face. Her family was aware of the abuse but no one saved her from this situation; however, she felt that she was worth being saved. As she continued to talk about her situation, tears ran down my cheeks. I began to think about how I had been used and taken advantage of in the past. Watching that show reinforced the fact that I do not have to feel guilty anymore about the things that happened to me, and that I too, am worth being saved!

The abuse the contestant experienced as a child was no different than what happened to me. It was easy for me to see how she needed to give her all in the competition in order to win but in that same light, I also needed to realize that I needed to do better in my own life. I could see there was no need for the guilt she was holding onto from her childhood and on into her adult life. It was time she took advantage of the opportunity she was being given through this competition.

Her situation was much like what we face every day when we wake up in the morning. We need to seize the day and avoid holding onto past guilt we feel. I later learned that with God there is no guilt or shame.

Sometimes I do not even realize that my main accuser is 'myself'. Once I had to travel out of the country for my job for 3 weeks when my daughter was only 17 months old. My biggest fear was that she was going to miss me, or even worse, forget who I was while I was gone. I was feeling guilty well before I even left the country! I began to blame myself for the job I had and for applying for this class when I knew about the 3 week travel requirement. I even began blaming myself for the move my family made to California, a place where we did not know anyone.

The guilt only made me feel worse and it did not help anything or anyone. It did not magically make the requirement for my class go away. As it turned out, I could not even enjoy the few weeks I had left with my daughter and the rest of my family. This way of thinking is counterproductive. This guilt is not something God wants me to live with whatsoever. There have been other times in my life where I unnecessarily felt guilty. In fact when I was raped I blamed myself for my 'part'. Little did I know, I did not play a 'part'. There was no point in any one of those scenarios where I requested my perpetrators to violate me? Those words never came out of my mouth, so it does not matter how I ended up alone with the person, what I was wearing, how flirty I was being, how much I did not fight back, nor how much I didn't say. None of those things matter. I can replay the situations over and over and over again or play the 'what if?' game, but I in no way asked anyone to take advantage of me. What happened was not my fault. I did not deserve anything that happened to me and that guilt is not mine to carry!

Did some disturbing things happen to me? Yes. If I would have been more cautious and less naïve would I have been in some of those situations? No. But I was not aware I needed to be cautious. I was ignorant and naïve so I mistakenly put myself in situations some would consider dangerous. Now I know that some people have evil intentions and not everyone has my best intentions at heart but this fact is not my fault. It is bad enough that I have to deal with what those perpetrators did to me, the last thing I need to do is feel guilty it even happened to me. I was not at fault... I am blameless and should feel blameless!

From Lonely to Comforted

"Come near to God and he will come near to you..."

James 4:8

One of darkest periods in my life came after the second time I was raped. I was a freshman college student and I was no longer around my family, who loved and cared for me unconditionally. I found myself alone in a new world with new friends and some superficial relationships.

I felt misunderstood and trapped without transportation to get away from the people I felt judged me. I could not just sit in my room at night because all I wanted to do was cry, scream, and even to die sometimes. I would take walks by myself and when people saw me walk in the door, their first assumption was that I had been out with some man. I would hear them talking about how freshmen girls did not know how to handle the new freedoms that come with college life and how freshmen girls start doing any and everything with anybody. Little did they know, I was merely a freshman girl that had recently been taken advantage of, yet I had no one to talk to while their judgmental opinions loomed over my head.

It was a lonely time in my life... My old high school friends were either enjoying their college experiences at their respective schools or still basking in their senior year of high school, thus leaving me feeling even more alone.

Back then, there were always a lot of people around me. Looking back, I wish I would have buried myself in my books but I could not stay in a quiet place for long periods of times. My thoughts seemed to consume me. So instead of feeling alone I looked for various forms of distractions. From the outside, I felt that I must have looked like easy prey because many men tried to get my attention. Most of the time I ignored these men and denied passing out my phone number, even when they only made a request for a simple date.

There was however one man in particular that came with something I could not reject; it was the Word of God. I was enamored with the way he knew scripture and how he used the Word of God in order to speak to me. Unfortunately because he was a physical presence in my face, I had the misconception that this man was good for me. We began to start a relationship and soon after married.

My loneliness clouded my judgment... even though I noticed signs that our relationship was unhealthy, I still continued to listen to him. I did not want to be alone nor did I want to feel that pain again. Unknowingly all I did was switch from one

26

form of pain to another and in the end, my feelings of loneliness returned anyway.

During my journey I realized that I had let other things take the place of God in my life. At times, they were sinful things like drinking, clubbing, and men. At other times, they were not so overly destructive and in fact may have even been considered good things like ministry and volunteer work but they were not what God wanted from me during that season. No matter what those 'things' were, none of them could fill the empty feeling I had deep down within my inner being nor make me feel less alone.

Later, I subconsciously developed a philosophy and an expectation to be available for anyone I came into contact with in the same way I wanted them to be supportive of me. I would latch onto anyone who had free time and engulf myself in whatever they had going on, just to escape my own world. Of course I always ended up being disappointed.

It was not until I first reflected on my own life that I realized what I really knew all along... there was someone who was faithful to me my entire life. I cannot think of a time when I felt God had left me alone. Now there have been times in my life when I have felt extremely close to God and there have been other times when I felt like I have been in a long-distance relationship with Him.

Those long-distance periods were crucial times only because I still knew that God and I had a relationship even though I had no close contact with Him. I had no idea where our relationship exactly stood or what direction I should go in. I had been involved in long-distance relationships in my past and if I went one day without talking to my significant other, it was a problem. So how much more important was it to avoid neglecting my personal relationship with God.

Honestly, when it came to long-distance relationships, I felt if the guy and I did not have daily contact there was really no need to continue the relationship. If I had not received a call by the time I ate lunch, I had a problem with my significant long-distance other and I would call him with an attitude wondering why he had not called me to check to see how my day was going. It was bad enough not having the guy around but when you add in the fact that I already suffered some extremely lonely days, it was not a good mix... plus there were always other people who were interested in filling that space for me.

There are many other things that work to fill that 'space' during those distant times from God. These 'space fillers' can be people, work, hobbies, and even work we do for God. My biggest 'space filler' tends to vary from one thing to another. I often ask myself, why are these 'space fillers' infiltrating my life? If I did not allow a 'space filler' to come in between a relationship I had with a guy, why would I allow this to happen with God?

You would think that I would do everything in my power to search for God to find out what He has for me. Because in Him there are so many things I need in my life - healing, peace, and joy. How can I ever achieve these things if I am more worried about the 'space fillers'?

Nevertheless, when it comes to the relationship I have with God, I sometimes have an attitude of well God what you require of me is just too much for me to handle. Do you realize how much I have to do today? This week? This month? This year?

Fortunately the best thing about God is that He does not necessarily try to contact me with the same attitude I had when I felt I was being ignored. It is always in a gentle manner, in a whisper, in a loving manner which at times seems to be easy to overlook and ignore. No one likes to be ignored, not even God. So sometimes He takes it up a notch to get your attention and make you desperate for Him but it is never meant to destroy you.

God has always been there, especially during those times I really needed Him. It was not until I was truly delivered that the void I felt finally filled up. And this was without any outside 'space filler'. I no longer felt the feeling of loneliness I had

carried for so long... I began to feel comforted as I drew closer
to Him and Him to me.

What Happened to You Does Not Define You

Sometimes it is hard for a person to accept that they were raped, molested, or taken advantage of. There are strong feelings and emotions associated with the incident but those feelings are different for everyone. However, it is important to remember that those terrible things that happened to you, do not define you.

One day I was at work and a co-worker told me a beautiful story. He first asked me whether I had ever heard of the Japanese word *Kintsugi*. I had not, so he went on to explain that *Kintsugi* is a type of pottery which dates back to the 15th century in Japan. It is further described as when broken pieces of pottery are mended with gold, silver, or platinum powder. Once the pottery is fixed, it is regarded as having a higher value than it originally had, especially since it had been previously broken.

In that same light, if you have been sexually assaulted, the reality of it will never change but it does not have to define who you are as a person. You cannot change the fact that it happened, and it may have led to feelings of low self-esteem or perhaps even feeling dirty but these feelings do not make you.

Because this happened to you, you may now be a little different but sometimes it's that difference in you that will actually make you of more value than you were before.

From Worthless to Valuable

"I praise you because I am fearfully and wonderfully made; your works are wonderful, I know that full well."
Psalm 139:13-15

When I was taken advantage of, the first thing I wanted to do was take a shower to wash and scrub my whole body. I felt the dirtiest I had ever felt in my life. I even wanted to wash off the filth that consumed my inner being. As I showered, I wanted the water to rinse away the tears that flowed down my cheeks along with the grime from the man who had attacked me. However, no matter how many times I washed my body nor how long the shower, nor how hot the water was, I still felt dirty and used.

I also felt feelings of worthlessness. After people experience a sexual assault, many begin to feel they are damaged goods and that their worth has diminished. You ultimately feel violated and that perhaps you are no longer good enough for a true relationship, marriage, or for anything else because you are no

32

longer 'pure'. Even more hurtful was how some people would try to help me by saying that it was not about the sexual act but it was all about control.... This made me feel even more like a doormat. It was as if they were saying I was merely something someone could simply throw away once they were done with their "business" and had proven their point of control.

One day I was watching a weight-loss television show. On the show was a client who had always been overweight. He had also been in a car accident where he ended up losing an arm at the site of the crash. After the accident, he ended up quitting school and moving back in with his parents. He had lost all hope and simply slept all day every day; he actually said that he felt like he was damaged goods. This feeling stemmed from the fact that he did not feel accepted just because something about him was clearly different than other people.

One time I was in a relationship with someone who was trying to continuously control me in everything I did. He knew about my past because I had confided in him but he would often tell me that I should be glad God wanted him to be with me because I was damaged goods and not many people could deal with the problems I had since I had been raped. Those were lies from the pit of hell!

These types of feelings are the complete opposite of what God has for you no matter what experiences you have encountered. Just because someone violated your body does not devalue you! Your value is the same as it was pre-violation. I am still the same person I was prior to any bad situation that happened to me. The attacks I have experienced do not define me. I am not just that girl who got raped. I am more than that. I am that young lady who is a survivor of sexual assault.

I do not nor cannot totally disregard what has happened to me in the past, but I have to continue to press on towards the goals God has set for me and I know He has great things for me. I do not believe that I am damaged goods because God does not invest in the damaged goods business. I may have had bad things happen to me but I have risen out of the ashes and I will succeed and I will have the life God has destined for me. I will be positive. I will not live in fear.

There were many fears that arose as a result of my un-wanted attacks, whether fear of someone attacking me or fear from pursuing my dreams, or even fear from living in freedom and without worry. However I will be God's revived goods and I will use my voice to be a blessing to others who come in my path.

I was doing my hair one morning and I needed to see the back so I got a handheld mirror to see better. My eyes went directly to a scar on my neck about the size of my thumb. I cringed because it had been a while since I had seen this scar. I actually smiled after about 10 seconds because I remembered when I got the scar and how I received a beautiful blessing right after. I got the scar during training for work. At first I was embarrassed and wanted to hide it because it was ugly. About two weeks later I found out I was pregnant with my beautiful baby girl.

I was no longer concerned about that ugly scar anymore. Every once in a while someone would ask me what happened and when asked I would initially be confused because I had forgotten about the scar altogether. That is also how it is when it comes to mental scars in our lives. At first when something traumatic happens, we are embarrassed and try to conceal what has happened to us simply because we feel that what happened to us defines us. But then God steps in and our focus turns to heavenly things. Our focus changes and sometimes we even forget we have that old scar.

At times we may be reminded of what happened to us but then we have a war story to tell. People will be able to see that in spite of the story, God has pulled us through the hard times. Therefore there is no need to conceal what happened because we are healed. My scar may be a little lighter and smaller now but it is still there; however, it no longer hurts and it has only served to have made me stronger! I truly believe that because I am in His hands, I am more valuable now than ever before!

From Depression to Joy

*"When the righteous cry for help, the LORD hears
and delivers them out of all their troubles."*
Psalms 34:17

Depression hit me like a brick wall soon after I was attacked. It felt as though there was a dark cloud overshadowing and consuming me no matter where I went. Along with this cloud came an overwhelming sense of sadness. In the face of others, I tried to smile and give off the aura of happiness in order to overcompensate for the hurt I felt inside, when in reality I just wanted to stay in bed and cry the entire day.

There were days when my will to live was completely sapped. Although I never formed a plan on how to take my life, I would think to myself that if I did not wake up the next morning, I would be happy. I was so tired of feeling so bad. I was no longer interested in doing the things I normally wanted to do such as visiting with friends or talking on the phone. I also despised being at home but I lacked the energy to leave my house... I was in a lose-lose situation.

36

As we take another look at Tamar's life, she became a recluse because she felt her life was over after her brother raped her. There have been many times in my life when I could truly relate to Tamar, because I have wanted to give up on my dreams and my life just like she did. Crawling in the bed and not interacting with anyone in the outside world sounded like the best idea for my future. All of my hope was gone and my life had no purpose.

I even tried to get professional help but I think I was a master at masking my true feelings. I somehow managed to avoid setting off any red flags with my counselors. During my sessions, the counselors would say I was handling the things that happened to me extraordinarily well while internally, I knew I was not handling anything well. I secretly wanted to die.

I felt as though because I felt like nothing, I must be nothing; however, those feelings of nothingness never told the real truth. I have learned that no matter what happens to me, God has a plan for my life and nothing will disrupt His plan. I have to be secure in my thoughts knowing that regardless of what happens, I am somebody and I have a purpose to be here on this earth, no matter how I might be feeling.

Knowing God has a plan for me gives me joy. Now I am able to get up every morning and go on with my day because I know He has a plan for me. Now I must simply walk in that plan He set for me. I have no reason to be sad because everything I need is taken care of. I have no reason to be depressed because God has all of my concerns taken care of.

Once I embraced this truth, the fog that surrounded me lifted and I was able to see what was around me. Only then did I gain the ability to see the path I could take in my life. Some of the things I used to enjoy doing changed but at least I finally had some hobbies again. I also wanted to be around the right people who loved me and encouraged me to be the best me that I could be. In those times when I find that cloud reforming, I simply reflect on the original plan that God has laid out for me and my joy rises again.

From Unrest to Peace

"And the peace of God, which transcends all understanding, will guard your hearts and your minds in Christ Jesus."
Philippians 4:7

Following the incidents I disclosed, I felt a variety of feelings which led to complete unrest, especially inside of my head. It was hard for me to concentrate on my daily routine. This unrest affected my entire life. From 1993 until 2010 I continuously said that there was one thing I wanted in my life and it was 'true peace'.

What Happened to You Does Not Define You

There were times when I suffered from insomnia. At night my mind seemed to wonder into deep thinking about what I should have done or what I could have done differently. I would also play out alternate scenarios while imagining how my life would be different... how I would most likely be in a better place... and how I would feel at peace. I usually wanted to disappear from my current life and travel around the country just to satisfy a need I felt deep within me. This would also serve as an attempt to escape from the reality of my life.

Unfortunately, this escape only gave me a false sense of reality. I was unable to feel any true satisfaction nor could I exhale and just simply 'be'. I felt as though my mind was always racing and I could not seem to get a handle on my feelings. Everything was always in disarray. I felt helpless and could not find any type of order. I would only get glimpses of peace, which sadly, only lasted a moment.

In my head, I would picture peace as a torrential rain-storm in the woods with the rain beating down heavily along with lightning and thunder. In the midst of the storm, I see myself sitting in a small nook on the side where there is a covered area. Even with the vicious storm raging around me, I am safe... not even one raindrop can reach me. I can hear the rain but cannot be touched by it. Ironically, from my perspective, I actually see the beauty of the storm because I see the positive aspect of the rain, which is producing growth.

If I were out in the rain, I would be uncomfortable, wet, and scared. However, God represents the cover I see provided in my vision. I can rest or hide in Him and no matter what is going on, it does not affect me in any way. The storm is only producing growth in me. I am now able to have the proper perspective and see the true purpose behind what is happening.

In order to see things from this particular perspective, I had to completely shift my way of thinking. I had to acknowledge that God is in control and that no matter what happened in my life or what happens from this point on, He is in control. I realized that everything that happens to me will be handled as long as I am with Him.

So many times in my life I have had too much going on and these things prevented me from reaching the level of peace I yearned for. When I lived in California, I visited a neighbor in her home. She had the exact same layout as my house but as I entered her home I felt a sudden peace. It was because it was open and there was a place for everything. When my husband and I got married we did not get rid of anything. We tried to consolidate all of our belongings and our home looked cluttered.

As soon as I left my neighbor's house, I went back home and started to donate items we did not need. I also made sure that everything in our home had a certain place. Afterwards our home became a peaceful place to live in. Just like my home, I needed to unclutter my mind. Thinking about the 'What Ifs?' does not fix any mistakes I made nor does it erase any of the situations that happened to me in the past.

Just like I have my reference point of being in the woods with the comfort I get seeing how in the midst of the storm I remain dry while everything around me is drenched, I praise the Lord. I see that even through the storm I am untouched and blessed. I praise the Lord because I know that no matter what I have been through, I can still have peace. God is still looking after me and I am covered by Him. I can no longer wander in the woods looking for a refuge because He is my refuge. I praise God because I have found Him and with Him I have gained a measure of 'true peace' that surpasses all understanding.

Fight for Your Healing

In the Bible there is a story of a woman who had an issue of blood for 12 years. She went through a process looking to be healed but nothing she tried seemed to work. Finally she hears about a man by the name of Jesus. She heard He was healing people and she wants to find this man with healing power. She must have felt that if He can heal all of those other people, He could do the same thing for her! She had to have been weak because she had been bleeding for years. She used whatever remaining energy she had to push to reach Jesus and receive her healing. She made her way through the crowd with enough faith to know that all she needed to do was simply touch the hem of Jesus's garment and she would receive the healing she had been searching for over the last 12 years. After her fight to get to Him, she received healing in an instant.

I had some friends that were doing weekly conference calls for the public which were designed to encourage people. One day we had a snow day from work and I was listening into the show. One of the speakers said sometimes you have to actually fight for your healing. This resounded within me because I had never looked at healing as something I was required to fight for... I always thought it just happened.

At that very moment, I realized fighting for my healing was exactly what I had to do in order to reach the point of transitioning from a victim into a survivor. Sometimes you have to push through all of the adversity standing up against you. My biggest enemy has been myself, and I mistakenly let what happened in my past define me. I had to forgive the people who violated me. I know most of the time when a person does not forgive another, the only person hurt is the person who does not forgive. The people I failed to forgive did not even know I was mad at them and while I lied awake at night, they slept just fine.

One person who raped me continued to talk to me every time we saw each other. I would ignore him but internally I would be so angry. Finally, one day I had enough and yelled at him. I asked him, why did he keep talking to me? He looked confused so I told him, you know that you raped me. He genuinely looked confused. He said that he was drunk and did not remember anything that happened that night. I explained to him what happened and he profusely apologized. As hard as it was, I forgave him in that moment because I wanted to be free even more than remaining angry at him.

I had to let go then push and fight for my healing. It took courage to forgive and I had to be strong but it was not easy. It was so much easier being mad and bitter but those feelings were only hurting me. When I think of the pain associated with sexual assault, I cringe because it is unexplainable. However, anyone who has fallen victim to sexual assault can overcome the pain and fight for their healing.

From Fear to Courage

"So do not fear, for I am with you; do not be dismayed, for I am your God. I will strengthen you and help you; I will uphold you with my righteous right hand."

Isaiah 41:10

When I was attacked, I felt like if I fought back there was a possibility I would lose my life. During the acts I was terrified and just froze. I silently wanted the attacks to just be over. The fear of losing my life is something I never want to feel ever again in my life. This fear was implanted deep within me and never left. Since then, the fear has built up more, has consumed me, and has even infiltrated other areas of my life.

When I was attacked, the surmountable amount of fear I felt was natural. Unfortunately that fear transferred to almost every other part of me - physically, emotionally, and even spiritually. I was afraid to be myself or to do anything. When I would be out walking, I would constantly look behind me, beside me, and in front of me to make sure I was not being followed. Even though my attackers were people I knew, I became ever more afraid of strangers. As for the people I knew, I was not only scared of them physically but also emotionally.

This fear kept me from doing things spiritually. I never felt comfortable delving into a close relationship with God. Even when I knew God was calling me to do certain things... because of fear, I did not want to walk in obedience. In fact, this very book was a part of that fear. The fear kept me from doing things I previously enjoyed like riding on airplanes, roller coasters, and the list goes on and on. I wanted to pursue many activities but once it came time to actually leave the house, I simply could not. At the time, I honestly did not realize why I no longer wanted to participate in the activities that used to be normal for me. Fear is not of God. It has been a journey and sometimes I have to remind myself that I do not need to be fearful of anything because perfect love drives out fear and that kind of love comes from God.

Finally, I realized that I was at a crossroads... I could either choose to live in bondage, sickness, or as a victim or I could live free, healed, and as a survivor without fear. As soon as I decided to give up the fear and trust in the power of God, I finally could live. I began to recollect those things I was terrified of doing and I soon began to realize those dreams. The fear never consumed me and I was able to regain the courage to walk into the life God called me to live, regardless of my past.

From Anger to Forgiveness

"Do not take revenge, my dear friends, but leave room for God's wrath, for it is written: 'It is mine to avenge; I will repay,' says the Lord."
Romans 12:19

After being violated, I eventually got angry, no very angry. I wanted every attacker, well at least anyone who had ever done anything to hurt me in my past to pay for what they did to me. It got to the point that whenever I would even come across someone who reminded me of people who had hurt me, I would automatically have a brewing stir within me... I wanted to lose it and fly off the handle.

I wanted to yell, scream or just be violent towards anyone who was around. I was harboring bitterness within my inner being. I felt my anger was 100% justified and that no one could take that away from me. My innocence had already been taken, my dignity had already been taken, so much of me had already been taken but I was determined to hold on to my anger! I did not consciously decide not to forgive my attackers but

47

forgiving them was certainly not a priority. I had already heard it was important to forgive people for what they do to us because God forgives us. In most cases this would be fine but this was my body which was violated along with my trust. People took advantage of me in a way that is hard to explain thus causing deep pain within me, which was slowly eating me alive.

I was holding on to my anger because it was something I could control, which was a commodity I had lost during my attacks. Yet, the very thing I was holding onto was causing me even more pain. I had to truly forgive my attackers and in doing so, I could be freed. I eventually wrote a letter to not only my attackers but to all the other people in my life whom I felt had hurt me in any way. I told them my true feelings, how what they did to me made me feel but at the end of the letter I forgave them. When I pressed send on the Facebook messages and emails I felt an overwhelming sense of relief within me... I was no longer harboring what happened to me.

I remember one day I was picking my daughter up to put her in bed when I accidently pressed some buttons on the television remote. The channel changed to a cinema channel talking about all of the movies available on the pay-per-view channels. These movies are generally the ones which recently left theaters but there was one trailer that caught my attention. At the beginning, there was a disclaimer stating all parents should cover their children's eyes and ears before even playing the trailer for the movie.

This piqued my curiosity because it was just a trailer and I wondered what could be so bad about a trailer. It turned out that the movie was about a young woman who gets raped and then seeks revenge on those who violated her. My initial gut reaction was – "GET THEM!" I mentally cheered the woman on as she attacked her assailants but then I caught myself. I suddenly remembered the scripture where the Lord says vengeance is His. If I truly believe in His Word, I know I do not have to do anything, nor does my family have to do anything to get back at my attackers. I must admit that this is not easy because I sometimes want the people who made me hurt, to hurt also.

Fortunately I have learned to focus on the One who has the ultimate power, which supersedes any other power found here on earth. This power can heal my broken heart, my broken body, and my broken spirit. This power God has given to me to regain my voice. When I was being violated, I did not have a voice at all. I did not ask to be raped or sexually assaulted but I eventually decided that I will not continue to allow my attackers to have control over my life. Perhaps they had it for a moment but they no longer get any more seconds of my life to control. I have decided to release the anger within me and allow God to take complete control. I had to make the decision to let go and let God take care of the people who violated me.

One person I could not forget to forgive was me, Samantha. Sometimes I replay being attacked over in my head and I reflect on where I could have done something, anything differently. I could have yelled louder, or not froze up, or hurt the attacker in some kind of way to get out of the situation. This is a classic case of the saying "hindsight is 20/20". I finally realized that it is easy to see after the situation has occurred, what I could have done differently but in the present, it was an absolute must to forgive myself and not be mad anymore so I could move on with my life.

From Distrust to Trust

"But I trust in you, LORD; I say, 'You are my God.'"
Psalms 31:14

I did not have any levels of trust for anyone after I was raped. I lost hope in society. I did not believe that there was anyone out there who truly wanted the best for me. This began to show up in all of my relationships. I was afraid to love. I had formed a complete barricade around my heart, which eventually extended throughout all of me. At first no one was allowed inside but after a while I did allow some people into the first 'level' of my fabricated heart security system. Those people included some family members, my husband, and a few very select friends.

When I think about trust, it reminds me of the stories my husband told me about his military training. One day he told me about being attacked by an enemy; if you are in a formation, you are trained not to necessarily focus on the threat right in front of you. The person beside you is responsible for what is directly in front of you and vice versa. Therefore you have to place a great deal of trust in someone else because their accuracy and skill may determine whether or not you will live. Can you imagine the camaraderie that develops from this type of training and experience? Your focus is neither on yourself nor what is going on right in front of you but instead it is on protecting another person beside you. And if you take your focus off of what is in front of them and switch the focus to yourself, you both could possibly be hurt or even worse killed.

The one thing I realized is I can always put my trust in God. He is always trustworthy, always looking out for our good, and He would never let anything happen to us that is not supposed to happen. This is refreshing to know; so we do not have to be fearful of doing whatever it is He has called us to do. When I would first meet a person, I would let them know I had trust issues. It was not because of anything they did but it was due to my past experiences, which led to my hesitation in trusting anyone. I was prepared for people in my life to let me down. I was unable to expect the best in them because I saw the worst happen so often. It may be hard to believe but all it took was for God to step in and my whole life was changed... I could openly trust again.

My Healing

"And we know that in all things God works for the good of those who love him, who have been called according to his purpose."
Romans 8:28

When I initially began to write this book, I was still in the healing process from the sexual assaults I had endured in my life. I was simply trying to just 'make it' through my everyday life and my only remaining hope was in God. 20 years after my first attack I made a decision on Valentine's Day to follow God wholeheartedly. I was in the process of moving from California to Maryland. During this transition, my daughter and I stopped at my dad's house in Kentucky.

On this particular Valentine's Day, I was away from my husband. I was not sad but I began to reminisce about my life. I decided that it was time for me to completely turn my life over to God and surrender everything to Him. I was tired of the yo-yo effect on my life. I would spend my time doing things I wanted to do and would add God into the equation later. I could see that this equation never seemed to add up. I could never seem to feel completely at peace nor experience a full measure of joy while fighting to be normal and okay.

When I prayed to the Lord this time, I knew He was going to send me to a ministry that would provide a church family for me; a family that would lead me into a place I had never been in my life with God. Before I even arrived in Maryland, a friend of mine had already begun inviting me to her church. I decided to go to a Bible Study at the church and although most of the lesson was over my head, I liked the fact that I felt I could grow there. The following Sunday, I attended their Worship Service. My daughter was comfortable with all of the members and I felt like I was at home. I even sang in the choir the first Sunday as a visitor.

As I continued to attend the church, I learned more about the freedom there is in Christ and how I no longer needed to live in bondage because of the things that happened to me in the past. I saw how people would pray and how people were delivered just like I read about in the Bible. To be honest, initially I was scared and did not understand exactly what was going on but I knew I wanted that same type of healing from God. I had always believed that the same type of healing I read about in the Bible could really happen today because God has not changed.

Even after I got settled in, there were still times I did not want to go to church on Sundays for Worship Service or Wednesdays for Bible Study but I continued to press on and go. And each time I would attend it was as though the lesson was tailored just for me. There was one Wednesday when all of the women prayed for my hurt because I shared about the pain I carried from my past experiences and relationships. On another night following a Bible study, I talked to the First Lady of the church and told her that there were times I felt sick to my stomach and I did not know why. She explained that it was because I was close to my deliverance. She also added, on the end of the conversation, that I was going to be able to finally trust my husband, which I felt was impossible considering how vast the lack of trust was at the time.

While in the moment, I did not know what the First Lady really meant but I was ready for all of the baggage I carried to be lifted. I knew I had tried everything else but the only One who could do it for me was God. On May 27th the sermon was on deliverance and the minister went on to describe ways to reach deliverance through Christ. I went up for the altar call to declare that I wanted to be delivered.

First a minister in the church prayed for me then the next thing I knew people were surrounding me on all sides. When I came to myself, it was 3 hours later but it felt like it had only been about 15 minutes. I felt completely different! I was healed and delivered then came the cherry on top... the First Lady said I still had a hip problem. I knew I had not told her that 7 years earlier I was struck by a car in a parking lot. I was actually told by a neurologist that I could expect to be in a wheelchair at some point in my life because I had permanent nerve damage. I had been in some level of pain since the day I was hit by the car.

Once the women prayed for me again, specifically for my hip, I suddenly felt a tingling in my leg. I then realized that my leg was healed and I had no more pain. Afterwards I also felt feelings of calmness come over me. I felt a sense of peace that I had never felt in my life. Even better, I began to trust my husband and everyone else around me again. The walls I had built around my heart crashed to the ground. I was open to love!

The pain I felt in the past was simply washed away and I no longer felt the intense pain I had been carrying around. I was healed. I was delivered. I noticed that my relationship with others changed significantly, especially with my husband. Our relationship was 10 times better all because something changed inside of me. I finally found my voice. I knew at that point, my journey of restoration could begin and I could help others reach the same point of healing.

Your Voice

"My flesh and my heart fail; but God is the strength of
my heart and my portion forever."
Psalms 73:26

One day I was watching a weight-loss television show and a contestant on the show was being eliminated. The host wrapped her arms around the contestant and said that her mother said obstacles are only speed bumps. This story reminds me of an old apartment complex I used to live in where there were a lot of speed bumps. The speed bumps were there to slow cars down to avoid drivers speeding in areas where pedestrians may be present.

I have a problem with these speed bumps because I always drive over them a little slower than I normally drive but far from the normal complete stop my husband makes. He always complained when I went over the speed bump and warned me about tearing my car up. I would roll my eyes because I have been driving for over 10 years and this set of speed bumps were not my first speed bumps and nothing had torn up yet.

Looking back at the situation reminds me how I tackle speed bumps in my life. Some people will allow life to come to a complete halt when adversity hits. I am far from saying I am completely unfazed by adversity but much like speed bumps, I get shook up a little bit but I know the shaking will only last a little while and then the smooth road is coming. Hallelujah!

Even though it may look as though there is no hope in a situation, 'but God'… Only those two words are necessary, 'but God'… Yes, He has stepped in every time I have gotten shaken up in this life… and yes there have truly been some times I was almost thrown out of the car, 'but God'… There were times I probably deserved to fail, 'but God'… There were times I was not obedient, 'but God'… Those speed bumps are only designed to slow us down and shake us up a little bit not completely bring our lives to a complete stop.

From just a speed bump, a car does not experience so much damage that it is impossible to continue driving. You have to keep going towards your destination and not give up on the vision God has given you for your life. Not only does your life depend on it, other people's lives do too. We have to remember that other people need us to rise up so they can learn how to get their healing and deliverance. We have to be a light, a glimmer of hope for someone that may be in a dark place.

These dark places include suicide, abuse, sickness, and anything that holds people back from walking in the glory of God.

My speed bumps have been rape, abuse, divorce, and many, many more but I have continued to press on in this race. Nothing can stand in the way of what God has for me. Sure, I have had setbacks but when it comes down to it, I know God is there and I know that regardless of what speed bump comes my way, I do have a voice. I refuse to live like Tamar and everyone else that has fallen victim of sexual assault can also become a sexual assault survivor.